GW01072002

Pilgrim

Property of
_____

Pilgrimages

_____

_____

_____

_____

_____

_____

> *Pilgrims are persons in motion - passing through*
> *territories not their own - seeking something we might call*
> *completion, or perhaps the word clarity, a goal to which*
> *only the spirit's compass points the way.*
> Reinhold Niebuhr - Religious Philospher

The term 'pilgrim' derives from the Latin word *peregrinus*
(*per*, through + *ager*, field, land), which means a foreigner,
a stranger, or someone on a journey..

You don't have a soul. You are a Soul. You have a body.
C. S. Lewis

Soulful travel, *a pilgrimage*, covers many aspects of human existence. It is not just a physical journey, but most importantly an inner journey. You depart from daily life to journey to a sacred place for a spiritual motive.

Sacred Sites - Invitations - Gateways

Throughout history, in every culture sacred places - *where the physical world meets the spiritual world.-* possess a unique attraction. These locations offer an invitation to spiritual change and provide the gateway to initiate this change. Millions like yourself, finding material answers inadequate, accept the invitation. As a pilgrim you seek meaning, healing, religious insights and affirmations. Your chosen sacred destination is the gateway for a life changing experience. You have a focus and attention that is different from a tourist. You seek answers to ultimate questions. As a pilgrim, you remove the constraints of ordinary life, so you experience the mysterious and the miraculous. Through meditation and prayer you unburden your mind, seek healing, give thanks and renew your faith. The rewards come just as much from the journey as the destination.

May the stars light your way and may you find the interior road. Forward! Irish pilgrim's prayer.

The Pilgrim's Way and Manner

Seek friendship.
Be kind and help those less fortunate.
Be grateful for those who help you.
Be respectful.
Welcome Serendipity - the unexpected.
Rethink personal relationships, goals and values. Seek new prespectives.

Use Your Imagination.
Be observant, listen and pay attention.
Know the history of your destination.
Use prayer and meditation.
Be honest with yourself.
Have faith.

Pilgrimage demands you are open to what God can do. You must be open to change. You must be active, engaged in and committed to the journey. You will meet the unexpected in all life's aspects: physical, social, political, economic, moral and spiritual. In all encounters remember the essence of the pilgrim spirit is trust.

Pilgrims are poets who create by taking jouneys.
Reinhold Niebuhr, Religious philospher

Pilgrimage and *The Secret*

Recently a book *The Secret* became an international best seller. Using *The Secret* people are said to achieve health, wealth and happiness. Simply stated *The Secret* is an ancient law of attraction. "Everything coming into your life you are attracting." It's attracted to you by virtue of the images you're holding in your mind. It's what you are thinking. *The Secret* has three requirements for the Law of Attraction - *Ask, Believe and Receive.*

For Christians *The Secret* was summarized 2,000 years ago in the New Testament passage -

Therefore I say unto you, What things so ever ye desire, when ye pray, believe that ye receive them, and ye shall have them. - Mark 11:24

The power of pilgrimage is that it puts *The Secret* into action. For over 5,000 years, millions of people from every culture have taken their deepest hopes and desires to a sacred place where they have faith that answers can be found.

"Do not say that it is impossible to receive the Spirit of God. Do not say that God does not manifest Himself to man. Do not say that men cannot perceive the divine light, or that it is impossible in this age! Never is it found to be impossible, my friends. On the contrary, it is entirely possible when one desires it".
St. Symeon, 11th Century

I am convinced that pilgrimage is still a bona fide *spirit-renewing ritual. But I also believe in pilgrimage as a powerful metaphor for any journey with the purpose of finding something that matters deeply to the traveller. With a deepening of focus, keen preparation, attention to the path and respect for the destination at hand, it is possible to transform the most ordinary journey into a sacred journey, a pilgrimage."*
Phil Cousineau, The Art of Pilgrimage

This Journal As A Tool For Clarity and Focus

A pilgrimage has six stages - *A Yearning - Preparation - The Journey - The Arrival - The Sacred Experience* and *The Return.* Organise this journal around these stages. Record your thoughts, goals and experiences for each stage.

This Journal As A Testament
Remember Your Experiences

On pilgrimage friendships are made, stories told, amazing sites visited and new understandings reached. By writing these down you preserve the spirit and memories of your journey. Rereading in the future will give you pleasure, comfort and spiritual strength.

Take care of all your memories. For you cannot relive them
Bob Dylan

THE YEARNING

*For in their hearts doth
Nature stir them so,
then people long
on pilgrmage to go,
And palmers to be
seeking foreign strands,
To distant shrines
renowned in sundry lands.*
Georffrey Chaucer
The Canterbury Tales

*I have treated many hundreds of patients. Among those in the
second half of life - that is to say, over 35 - there has not been one
whose problem that in the last resort was not finding a religious
outlook on life.* Carl Jung, Psychologist

*"The centre of me is always searching for something beyond
what the world contains,something transfigured and infinite- the
beatific vision - God,....it fills every passion that I have -
it is the actual spring of life within me."*
  Betrand Russell, Philospher

In our modern world there is abundant searching, we
google, visit chat rooms, twitter and blog. We read
horoscopes, hold special stones, *Feng Shui* our homes, visit
therapists, mediums, have plastic surgery, take drugs,
drink alcohol, it's an endless list. In the middle ages it was
simpler, people knew they were searching for God. As St.
Augustine wrote, *"Truly our hearts are restless until they
find their rest in you, O God."*
Goethe calls it the "holy longing". It is this desire that leads
to your holy quest, your pilgrimage. You realize you have
the need, the hope and faith that making a special journey
will transform your life.

  We thirst at first.
  Emily Dickinson

Notes:

*"The pilgrims's instinct is deep set in the human heart.
It is indeed an affair of the heart rather than the head."*
Evelyn Waugh

PREPARATION

The day on which one starts out is not the time to start one's preparations. Nigerian folk saying.

Once the yearning is recognised you must plan and clarify. What is your sacred cause, your purpose? Plan so you can achieve it.

Historically, pilgrimages were serious affairs covering long distances and taking months or even years. It was necessary to make detailed preparations for practical matters - paying bills, securing the house, making special family arrangements and learning as much possible about the "holy" destination and any special journey requirements.

There were also traditional clothes and accessories. These were a *"wide brimmed hat"* for sun and rain protection, a *"script"*, a small leather satchel or bag in which documents, money, food and souvenirs were kept, a *"staff"*, used as walking and climbing stick, as a pole for vaulting streams, and a weapon against fierce dogs and other animals, *a long coat* that could double as a blanket, *a water bottle* and most importantly *suitable shoes*.

Mental and spiritual preparation included the focusing of objectives, discussing the trip with fellow pilgrims and churchmen. These preparations strengthen the faith in oneself and one's beliefs. Use them and you develop a new mindset of great anticipation with a willingness to seek new experiences and high hopes that the journey will bring about physical and spiritual transformations.

"In the field of observation, chance favours the prepared mind.
Louis Pasteur

Notes:

Give me my Scallop shell of quiet,
My staffe of Faith to walke upon,
My Scrip of Joy, Immortal diet,
My bottle of salvation.
My Crowne of Glory, hopes true gauge,
and thus I'll take my pilgrimage
  Sir Walter Raleigh

"The practice of soulful travel is to discover the overlapping point between history and everyday life, the way to find the essence of every place, every day: in the markets, small chapels, out-of-the-way parks, craft shops. Curiosity about the extraordinary in the ordinary moves the heart of the traveller intent on seeing behind the veil of tourism."
Phil Cousineau, *The Art of Pilgrimage*

The journey allows you time to prepare for your arrival and provides a transition period. You can look at your life's realities from a different perspective and in a different context. In medieval times pilgrimages were long and difficult. Pilgrims found that by creating a daily rhythm of spiritual and physical habits the journey was made easier. Enjoy the camaraderie of fellow pilgrims, welcome surprises and adventures, be generous in aiding others, and accept difficulties as a part of the journey, learning lessons from hardships.

On a long journey of human life, faith is the best of companions; it is the best refreshment on the journey; and it is the greatest property." Buddha

Thoughts for the Journey

Common sense and good nature will do a lot to make the pilgrimage of life not too difficult. W. Somerset Maugham

"he who leaves home in search of wisdom walks in the path of God" Mohammad

"You cannot travel the path until you have become the path" Buddha

We are pilgrims on the earth and strangers; we have come from afar and we are going far." Vincent van Gogh

Aim at heaven and you will get earth thrown in. Aim at earth and you get neither. C. S. Lewis

Did not our hearts burn within us as He talked to us on the road?" Luke 24:32

It is the Lord who goes before you. He will be with you; he will not fail you or forsake you. Do not fear or be dismayed. Deuteronomy 31:8

Pilgrims on the road to Santiago de Compostela, notice the shells on backpacks. These are the symbol of this pilgrimage. Shell symbols are also found on inns and hostels along the way indicating places that welcome pilgrims. The Shell Oil logo derives from this tradition.

Notes:

Is not the all-powerful God the pilot and sailor of our boat? Leave it to him. He himself guides our journey as he wills.
St. Brendan

"We attribute much to chance meetings, refer to them as turning points in our life, but these encounters could never have occurred had we not made ourselves ready for them. If we possessed more awareness, these fortuitous encounters would yield still greater rewards. It is only at certain unpredictable times that we are fully attuned, fully expectant, and thus in a position to receive the favors of fortune. The man who is fully awake knows that every 'happening' is packed with significance." Henry Miller

What saves a man is to take a step. Then another.
C.S.Lewis

To get through the hardest journey you need take only one step at a time, but you must keep on stepping Chinese Proverb

Journey Lessons

"Joan, a woman with Downs Syndrome, always walked much slower than everyone else. At first that caused anxiety—'We've got to walk 20k by this evening—How will we ever get there?' But walking alongside Joan, and listening to her, I heard: 'Hello sun, hello tree, hello stone, hello birds'. Often Joan would stop and look for a long time at one thing, or have a little chat with herself. She was aware of everything around her, enjoying being in the open air, completely unconcerned for our deadlines and targets. And in this way, she was much more able to be aware of the gift of the earth, of the gifts of each moment along the way, than I was, with my constant goal-orientation and worry about getting somewhere else.

John, a man with severe learning disabilities, who walked with us, was just happy to walk, it didn't matter to him whether we were walking to Santiago or John O'Groats. The rhythm of the walking, being alive in his body, in the open air—that was what counted for him. .. John's lesson to us was that it is the walking—the being present in that moment—that matters. God is not far off at the end of our journey, he is present with us every step of the way. … For our little group of walkers and for many of those whom we met along the way, Joan and John became pilgrim teachers."

On the way to Santiago de Compostela, Hugh Nelson
the L'Arche Community, Lambeth, London

Yet the Lord pleads with you still: Ask where the good road is, the godly paths you used to walk in, in the days of long ago. Travel there and you will find rest for your souls.
Jeremiah 6:11

"Don't walk in front of me, I may not follow.
Don't walk behind me, I may not lead.
Walk beside me and be my friend." Albert Camus

Well I'm pressing on, Yes, I'm pressing on...
Shake the dust off your feet, don't look back
Nothing can hold you down, nothing that you can lack
Well I'm pressing on, Yes, I'm pressing on
To the higher calling of my lord.
Lyrics: "Pressing on", Bob Dylan

THE ARRIVAL

Jerusalem

This is a great moment, when you see, however distant, the goal of your wandering. The thing which has been living in your imagination suddenly becomes a part of the tangible world. Freya Stark

Notes

If you miss the moment, you miss your life. John Daido Loori

Santiago de Compostela

Faith is to believe what you do not see; the reward of this faith is to see what you believe. Saint Augustine

The Five Excellent Practices of Pilgrimage
Practice the arts of attention and listening.
Practice renewing yourself everyday.
Practice meandering toward the centre of every place
Practice the ritual of reading sacred texts.
Pracitice gratitude and praise singing.
Based on coversations of Confucius and Zi Zhang

Lourdes

"Take off your shoes, for the place on which you stand is holy ground" Exodus 3 : 5-6

Notes:

"The sense of treading ground made holy by past events is crucial. The experience of the pilgrim in actually walking in the way of others enables them to become a participant in all that has happened. The pilgrim becomes one with all who have gone before." Martin Robinson..

Glastonbury

I am certain of nothing but the holiness of the heart's affections and the truth of imagination - what the imagination seizes as beauty must be truth - whether it existed before or not. John Keats

Imagination

"I shut my eyes in order to see." Paul Gauguin
For Romans imagination was the "inner eye", allowing you to see what is invisible but is there. The philosopher Kant developed the idea of a "productive imagination in a perceptual experience." By productive he meant well informed. For you this means that the extraordinary powers embodied in sacred buildings and sites can be revealed for a personal, emotional experience. Your knowledge of local history provides the foundation on which your imagination builds mental bridges so you spiritually participate instead of just visit. Imagination is also a tool for your future. Visualize the life you want.

Imagine what is behind the presence at these wisdom sites and places of pilgrimage. Imagine that its presence demands yours... Has your amazement been amazed yet ?
Phil Cousineau

Veil of Virgin Mary Chartres

Chains of St. Peter, Rome

Handbone of John the Baptist, Istanbul

Relics - were at the heart of medieval pilgrimages. They are holy objects believed to have spiritual, healing energy stored in them - the power of the supernatural and the possiblity of miraculous cures. Often they were tangible remains of Saints - bones, clothing or objects that were made holy through contact with the Saints, the Virgin Mary, or Christ. Some of the more famous relics are the Shroud of Turin, the remains of St.James at Compostela, the skulls of the three Magi in Cologne, in Rome the remains of St. Peter and St.Paul and thorns from the Crown of Thorns at Notre Dame in Paris.

The belief of miracles through relics has biblical roots. There is the Old Testment story- Kings 13:14-21 of the man accidently put in the tomb of the prophet Elisha, who when his body touched the bones of the prophet sprang back to life. In Mark 5:28-34 a woman is healed by touching Jesus's cloak. In Acts 19:11-12 there is the description of the miracle healings by the handkerchiefs of St. Paul when they are given to the sick.

Try as you will, you cannot annihilate that eternal relic of the human heart, love." Victor Hugo

Faith is different from proof; the latter is human, the former is a Gift from God. Blaise Pascal

Notes:

Any relic of the dead is precious, if they were valued living." Emily Bronte

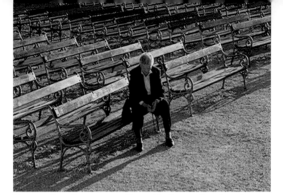

Prayer is when you talk to God; meditation is when you listen to God. ~ Anon

Prayer and Meditation

In a sacred environment, one has a unique opportunity of experiencing personal revelations, peace of mind, longed for healings, and what Henry Miller describes as "something beyond bliss."

Notes

Prayer does not change God, but it changes him who prays. Søren Kierkegaard

Pray, and let God worry. Martin Luther

Trouble and perplexity drive me to prayer and prayer drives away perplexity and trouble. Philip Melanchthen

Canterbury

We need to find God, and he cannot be found in noise and restlessness. God is the friend of silence. See how nature - trees, flowers, grass- grows in silence; see the stars, the moon and the sun, how they move in silence... We need silence to be able to touch souls.- Mother Teresa

Notes

Prayer may not change things for you, but it for sure changes you for things. Samuel M. Shoemaker

In the attitude of silence the soul finds the path in a clearer light, and what is elusive and deceptive resolves itself into crystal clearness. Mahatma Gandhi

"Eternal God, in whom mercy is endless and the treasury of compassion — inexhaustible, look kindly upon us and increase Your mercy in us, that in difficult moments we might not despair nor become despondent, but with great confidence submit ourselves to Your holy will, which is Love and Mercy itself." Closing prayer of The Chaplet of Mercy, Diary of Saint Faustina

"Miracles are not contrary to nature, but only contrary to what we know about nature." Saint Augustine

Miracles and Healing Every sacred destination has healing miracles associated with it - spirtual and physical. In truth, for some physical healing is the great motivation for pilgrimage. Historically these miracles were mainly in less scientific medieval times. In recent years, pilgrimage miracles have been associated with sacred sites where divine visions occurred like Lourdes or Knock. In rare cases sight is restored, the deaf can hear, the lame walk, cancer cells disappear. At Lourdes since 1947 a Catholic Church bureau uses strict medical criteria to examine miracles. The committee has examined 1,300 claims and presented 29 to the church, which recognized 19 as miracles. The reason most claims are not recognized is medicine was being taken or the original diagnosis was not authenticated or clear cut. Of course if you're healed these details are irrelevant. The real miracle is how every afflicted person feels strengthened and spiritually refreshed from a visit. Another truth discovered is how helping others less fortunate connects with healing yourself. In fellowship and aid to others personal problems often disappear. As Mother Teresa discovered when helping others *one can do anything with nothing,* arguably the true miracle.

"Back of every creation, supporting it like an arch, is faith. Enthusiasm is nothing: it comes and goes. But if one believes, then miracles occur." Henry Miller

We, the unwilling, led by the unknowing, are doing the impossible for the ungrateful. We have done so much, for so long, with so little, we are now qualified to do anything with nothing. Mother Teresa

Notes

Healing *may not be so much about getting better, as about letting go of everything that isn't you - all of the expectations, all of the beliefs - and becoming who you are.* Rachel Naomi Remen

When a cynical reporter found out Albert Einstein was religious he asked him if he believed in miracles. Einstein's response was *"show me something that isn't ."* .

Notes

"There are only two ways to live your life. One is as though nothing is a miracle. The other is as though everything is a miracle." Albert Einstein

The miracles of the church seem to me to rest not so much upon faces or voices or healing power coming suddenly near to us from afar off, but upon our perceptions being made finer, so that for a moment our eyes can see and our ears can hear what is there about us always. Willa Cather

"As for me, I know nothing else but miracles, Whether I walk the streets of Manhattan, Or dart my sight over the roofs of houses toward the sky, Or wade with naked feet along the beach just in the edge of the water, Or stand under the trees in the woods, Or talk by day with any one I love, Or sleep in bed at night with anyone I love, Or watch honey bees busy around the hive of a summer forenoon... Or the wonderfulness of the sundown, Or of stars shining so quiet and bright, Or the exquisite delicate thin curve of the new moon in spring... What stranger miracles are there?

Walt Whitman

The Return

*"Old things are past away, all's become new.
Strange! he's another man , upon my word...*
ending of John Bunyan's Pilgrim's Progress

A pilgrimage is a metaphor for life, your journey on earth in miniature. Lessons learned and transformations become part of who you are. Put your pilgrimage souvenirs in one special place and record your thoughts of this precious journey.

"Keep the pilgrim spirit always. Now go and live your lives without fear."
Santiago Cathedral, Bishop's blessing at end of 500 mile walk to - El Camino de Compostela.

Notes

You arrive where you started and know the place for the first time. T. S. Eliot

One cannot always be a stranger. I want to return to my homeland, make all my loved ones happy. I see no further than this. Albert Camus

"Lord, we ain't what we want to be; we ain't what we ought to be; we ain't what we gonna be, but, thank God, we ain't what we was." Prayer of former slave preacher.

Amazing Grace, how sweet the sound,
That saved a wretch like me...
I once was lost but now am found,
Was blind, but now, I see...
Through many dangers, toils and snares...
we have already come.
T'was Grace that brought us safe thus far...
and Grace will lead us home.

Amazing Grace, lyrics by John Newton (1725-1807)

Editors Note - The decorations on the side of pages are Illuminations from Medieval Bibles.
Published by Riverstone Publishing © R.Kihlstrom - rk@riverstoneplus.com